Five LOAVES and Two FISH

**Archbishop François-Xavier
Nguyen van Thuan**

Edited with and Introduction by Father John-Peter Pham

Morley ❖ Books

Witness to the Gospel, disciple of Jesus Christ, confessor to the faith—all of these titles describe Archbishop Francois-Xavier Nguyen van Thuan. He writes with a directness and an honest simplicity. Yet the power of his words show how prayer is possible even in the most difficult circumstances, how the reality of love can transform people's lives, and how even in the darkest moments the strength of God's presence can be felt.

This is a very moving book.

Francis Cardinal George, O.M.I.:
Archbishop of Chicago

To meet Archbishop Francis-Xavier Nguyen van Thuan is to be reminded of two great truths: that we live in a new Age of Martyrs, and that the martyrs are among the most joyful of Christians. The witness to Christ of this modern martyr-confessor, now a servant of the universal Church in Rome, is further proof that the Holy Spirit can transform impossibly difficult situations through the miracle of grace.

George Weigel, Author of *Witness to Christ: the Biography of Pope John Paul II*

Five LOAVES and Two FISH

This book has been translated already into seven
languages, and so I am grateful to Morley Books for
making it now available to English readers. The best
endorsement I can give is to repeat what the Holy
Father said after the Jubilee Year Lenten retreat in
the Vatican led by Archbishop van Thuan:

> "He himself was a witness to the Cross in
> the long years of his imprisonment in
> Vietnam and he frequently recounted to us
> the facts and episodes of his suffering in
> prison, thereby strengthening us in the con-
> soling certainty that when everything col-
> lapses around us and perhaps even within
> us, Christ remains our unfailing support."

Whoever wishes to draw profit from these words
should read carefully *Five Loaves and Two Fish*.

Bernard Cardinal Law
Archbishop of Boston

Cover and book design by Melanie Turner

First Edition

Morley Books
1814 1/2 N Street, N.W.
Washington, D.C. 20036

Library of Congress Cataloging-in-Publication Data

Nguyen van Thuan, François-Xavier Nguyen van Thuan, 1928–
    [Cinque pani e due pesci. Italian]
  Five Loaves and Two Fish/François-Xavier Nguyen van Thuan; edited
  with and introduction by John-Peter Pham.
  p.cm.
ISBN 0-9660597-5-1
    1. Christian Life—Catholic authors. 2. Nguyen van Thuan,
  François-Xavier Nguyen van Thuan, 1928– I. Title: 5 loaves and 2
  fish. II. Pham, John-Peter. III Title.

BX2350.2.N46716 2000
282'.597'09045—dc21

                                              00–038686

Printed in the United States of America

Title of the Italian original:

Cinque pani e due pesci

First published by Edizioni San Paolo, Milano (Italy), 1997.

Contents

INTRODUCTION
by Father John-Peter Pham

Archbishop François-Xavier Nguyen van Thuan was born in Huê, the ancient imperial capital of Vietnam, on April 17, 1928. He was ordained to the priesthood on June 11, 1953. After postgraduate studies in Rome, where he earned his doctorate in canon law, he served successively as a professor, spiritual director, and rector of the seminary in Huê, before becoming vicar general of the archdiocese. In 1967, at the age of thirty-eight, he was named bishop of Nha Trang in central Vietnam, by Pope Paul VI. He was consecrated bishop on June 24, 1968. His ministry as bishop of Nha Trang was an active one in those years after the close of the Second Vatican Council. In his diocese he actively promoted both vocations to the priesthood — nearly six hundred in the eight years of his episcopate — and religious life as well as the active involvement of the laity in pastoral councils and the social apostolate.

Outside his diocese, he chaired the Vietnamese Episcopal Conference's committee on development, a none-too-easy task in the midst of the war, and was named to serve on the Secretariat for the Laity at the Vatican. He was one of the founders of Radio Veritas, now based in Manila, the largest Catholic radio broadcasting system.

As the Vietnam War drew to a close with the communist invasion of the Republic of Vietnam, he was named by Pope Paul VI on April 24, 1975, to be coadjutor archbishop of Saigon, the capital of South Vietnam. The nomination of the popular prelate, however, was opposed by the new authorities, who arrested him on the Solemnity of the Assumption, August 15, that same year, placing him at first under house arrest. During this time, he secretly wrote a series of meditations to encourage his flock. Those meditations, smuggled out of his imprisonment and clandestinely published as *The Road of Hope,*[1] ensured in the coming years of his disappearance behind the walls of communist prisons that his voice would still be heard. Carried abroad by many of the "boat people," the text of *The Road of Hope* has been translated into more than a dozen languages and published worldwide as a testimony to the light, even amidst the darkness.

The archbishop was formally "arrested" on the vigil of the Solemnity of St. Joseph, March 18, 1976. On the Solemnity of All Saints, November 1, of that year, he was deported to North Vietnam in the hold of a tanker along with two thousand other political prisoners. The next decade of his life was spent in various prisons and "reeducation" camps of the communist regime, including nine years in isolation cells. Finally, under pressure from numerous international groups, the government formally released the archbishop on the Feast of the Presentation of the Blessed Virgin

[1] Archbishop François-Xavier Nguyen van Thuan, *The Road of Hope: Thoughts of Light from a Prison Cell*, translated with an introduction by Father John-Peter Pham (London: New City Press, 1997)

Mary, November 21, 1988, although it continued to prevent him from returning to his archdiocese and placed him under de facto house arrest in Hanoi, forbidden to celebrate the sacraments publicly. In the wake of the collapse of communism in central and eastern Europe, the nervous Vietnamese communist authorities expelled the archbishop in December 1991. Since then, he has lived in exile in Rome, traveling often to visit the dispersed members of his flock.

On the Feast of the Martyrs of Vietnam, November 24, 1994, Pope John Paul II named him the vice president of the Pontifical Council for Justice and Peace. On the Solemnity of the Birth of St. John the Baptist, June 24, 1998, the Holy Father elevated him to president of the council, whose function is to promote justice according to the Gospel and the social doctrine of the Church.

In addition to his work promoting Catholic social doctrine, Archbishop Nguyen van Thuan is well-known internationally as a spiritual director, retreat master, and preacher, whose ministry takes him to all continents every year. For the Great Jubilee of the Year 2000, Pope John Paul II invited the archbishop to preach the weeklong Lenten Retreat for the Holy Father, cardinals and bishops of the papal household, and the Roman Curia. The archbishop preached on the theme of "Witness to Hope."

This present book grew out of a series of reflections that, at the invitation of various bishops conferences, the archbishop prepared for World Youth Day 1997 in Paris, France. As it turned out, due to health reasons, the archbishop was unable to attend the event. The text of these reflections, interspersed with the intensely personal prayers composed by Archbishop Nguyen van Thuan during his captivity, nonetheless have value as the first time the archbishop, always a modest man, has publicly spoken at length of his long years as a silent witness to the faith.

Father John-Peter Pham, a priest of the Diocese of Peoria, Illinois, is the author of four books and numerous articles and reviews.

PREFACE

My dear young people,

Contemplating a beautiful panorama, the green hills and the blue sea with its white waves, makes me think of Jesus in the middle of the crowds. Looking at you face to face, with the eyes of Jesus, I say to you with all my heart: "Young men and women, I love you!"

In speaking to you today, I wish to take as my inspiration a passage from chapter six of St. John's Gospel. Stand up and listen to God's word:

Lifting up his eyes, then, and seeing that a multitude was coming to him, Jesus said to Philip, "How are we to buy bread so that these people may eat?" This he said to test him, for he himself knew what he would do. Philip answered him, "Two hundred denarii would not buy bread for each of them to get a little." One of his disciples, Andrew, Simon Peter's brother, said to him, "There is a lad here who has five barley loaves and two fish: But what are they among so many?" Jesus said, "Make the people sit down." Now there was much grass in the place; so the men sat down, in number about five thousand. Jesus then took the loaves, and, when he had given thanks, he distributed them to those who were seated; so also the fish, as much as they wanted. (Jn 6:5-11)

En route to the Jubilee of the Year 2000, are we seeking to discover who Jesus is, why we love him, how to let ourselves be loved by Jesus, until we come to follow him in the radicalness of our choices, with no thought for the length of the road, the exhaustion of the march under the summer sun, the absence of every comfort?

The Holy Father writes: "In communion with all the people of God who are on route to the Great Jubilee of the Year 2000, I would like to invite you this year to fix your gaze on Jesus, Teacher and Lord of our lives, meditating on the words recorded in St. John's Gospel: 'Teacher, where do you live?' 'Come and see' (Jn 1:38-39)" (*Message for World Youth Day XII, 1997*).

As a young man, then as a priest, and then again as a bishop, I have already traveled a part of the road, at times with joy, at times with suffering, even at times in prison — but always bearing in my heart an overflowing hope.

I felt a bit uncomfortable when they asked me to speak about my experience of following Jesus; it is not a nice thing to speak about oneself. But I remember that in the book *Les Imprévus de Dieu*, the author, the late Cardinal Suenens, asked Veronica: "You have allowed me to speak of your life only today; why did you not let me before? . . . . Because now I understand that my life does not belong to me, but it is all God's; God can do with it what he will for the good of souls." John Paul II has condensed this thought well in the title of his autobiography, *Gift and Mystery*, just as Mary did in her Magnificat.

Now then, my dear young people, I am following that passage in the Gospel, where Jesus offers five loaves and two fish. By themselves the loaves and the fish are nothing before a crowd of thousands of people, but it is all he has, and Jesus makes it his all; it is *gift and mystery*. Taking my cue from the boy in the Gospel passage, I will recall my experience in seven points: five loaves and two fish. It is nothing, but it is all I have. Jesus will do the rest.

Many times I suffer deeply because the mass media want to make me tell sensationalistic stories, to accuse, to denounce, to incite opposition, to seek revenge . . . This is not my goal. My greatest desire is to transmit my message of love, in serenity and truth, in forgiveness and reconciliation. I want to share with you my experiences: how I found Jesus in every moment of my daily existence, in discerning between God and God's works, in prayer, in the Eucharist, in my brothers and sisters, in the Virgin Mary, who was my guide along the way. Together with you I want to cry out: "Let us live the testament of Jesus! Let us cross the threshold of hope."

Rome, February 2, 1997,
Feast of the Presentation of the Lord

It is along the paths of daily existence that you can find the Lord! ...
This is the fundamental dimension of the encounter: it does not have to do with some thing, but with Someone, with the "One Who is Alive."

John Paul II,
Message for World Youth Day XII, 1997, *n. 1*

THE FIRST LOAF
Living the Present Moment

My name is Francis-Xavier Nguyen van Thuan, and I am Viêt-Nâmese, but in Tanzania and Nigeria, the youth call me Uncle Francis, which is a bit simpler, or, even better, just plain Francis.

Until April 23, 1975, I was, for eight years, bishop of Nha Trang, in central Viêt-Nâm, the first diocese entrusted to me, where I was happy and for which I will always keep a certain predilection. On April 23, 1975, however, Pope Paul VI named me coadjutor archbishop of Saigon. When the communists arrived in Saigon, they told me that this nomination was the result of a conspiracy between the Vatican and the imperialists to organize resistance to the communist regime. Three months later, I was summoned to the Presidential Palace, where I was placed under arrest: It was the day of the Blessed Virgin's Assumption, August 15, 1975.

That night, along the three hundred-mile road that brought me to my place of house arrest, many confused thoughts came to my mind: sadness, abandonment, exhaustion after three months of tension . . . But in my mind one word surged forth clear and bright to disperse all the darkness, the word of Bishop John Walsh, the famous Maryknoll missionary in China, spoken when he was freed after twelve years of prison: "I spent half my life waiting." It is very true: All prisoners, myself included, look forward to freedom every minute. But then I decided: "I am not going to wait. I will live each present moment, filling it to the brim with love."

It is not an unforeseen inspiration, but a conviction that had matured throughout my whole life. If I spend my time waiting, maybe the things I look forward to will never arrive. The only thing certain to arrive is death.

In the village of Cây-Vông, where I was kept under house arrest, under both open and secret surveillance by police mixed in with the people, day and night I found myself obsessed with the thought: My people! My people whom I love so dearly: a flock without a shepherd! How can I reach my people, in the very moment when they most need their pastor? The Catholic libraries have been confiscated, the schools closed, the sisters and religious who were teachers were being sent to work in the rice fields. The separation was a shock that destroyed my heart.

"I will not wait. I will live the present moment, filling it to the brim with love — but how?"

One night, a light came: "Francis, it is very simple. Do what St. Paul did when he was in prison: Write letters to the different communities." The next morning, in October 1975, I signaled to a seven-year-old boy, Quang, who was returning from Mass at five o'clock, when it was still dark: "Tell your mother to buy me some old pads of paper." Late that evening, when once again it was dark, Quang brought me the paper, and every night during October and November 1975, I wrote my message from captivity to my people. Every morning, the boy would come to pick up the pages and carry them home, where his brothers and sisters would copy them. That is how the book *The Road of Hope* came to be written. It was eventually published in eight languages: Viêt-Nâmese, English, French, Italian, German, Spanish, Korean, and Chinese.

God's grace gave me the energy to work and to go on, even in the most desperate moments. I wrote the book at night, in one and a half months, because I was afraid that I might not be able to finish: I was afraid of being transferred somewhere else. When I got to number 1001, I decided to stop; they are like the "A Thousand and One Nights" . . .

In 1980, when I was in forced residence in Giang-xá , North Viêt-Nam, I wrote (as before, at night and in secret) my second book, *The Road of Hope in the Light of God's Word and of the Second Vatican Council*, and then my third book, *Pilgrims on the Road of Hope*.

"I will not wait. I will live the present moment, filling it to the brim with love."

The Apostles had wanted to take the easy road: "Lord, send the people away, and they can find food . . ." But Jesus wants to act in the present moment: "Give them something to eat yourselves" (Lk 9:13). On the Cross, when the thief said to him, "Jesus, remember me when you come into your Kingdom," he answered, "Today you will be with me in Paradise" (Lk 23:42-43). In the word "today," we hear all the forgiveness, all the love of Jesus.

Father Maximilian Kolbe lived this radicalism when he would repeat to his novices: "Everything, absolutely, with no conditions." I once heard Dom Helder Camara say: "Life is learning to love." Once Mother Teresa of Calcutta wrote me: "What is important is not how many actions we perform, but the intensity of love that we put into each action."

How does one achieve this intensity of love in the present moment? I simply think that I must live each day, each minute as if it was the last one of my life. To leave aside everything accidental, to concentrate only on the essential. Each word, each gesture, each telephone call, each decision is the most beautiful of my life; I keep my love for everyone, my smile. I am afraid of wasting even one second by living it without meaning . . .

I wrote in the book *The Road of Hope*: "You have only one moment, and it is the most beautiful moment: the present moment (cf. Mt 6:34; Jn 4:13-15). Live it completely in the love of God. And if you build your life like a crystal from a million such sparkling moments, what a beautiful life it will be! Do you not see how easy it is?" (n. 997).

My dear young people, in the present moment Jesus needs you. John Paul II is calling you, insistently, to take up the challenge of today's world: "We live in an age of great transformations where ideologies that seemed destined to withstand the wear and tear of time are rapidly waning, on a planet where borders and frontiers are being redesigned. Humanity often finds itself uncertain, confused, and worried (Mt 9:36), but God's word does not wane; it runs throughout history, and amidst the changing events it remains stable and luminous (Mt 24:35). The faith of the Church is founded on Jesus Christ, the only savior of the world: yesterday, today, and for ever (Heb 13:8)" (*John Paul II, Message for the World Youth Day XII, 1997,* n. 2).

PRAYER
In Prison, for Christ

Jesus,

yesterday afternoon, Feast of Mary Assumed,

I was arrested.

Taken during the night from Saigon to Nha Trang

four hundred and fifty kilometers between two policemen,

I began the experience of a prisoner's life.

So many confused feelings in my head:

sadness, fear, tension,

my heart torn to pieces

for being taken away from my people.

Humiliated, I remember the words of Sacred Scripture:

"He let himself be taken for a criminal – et cum iniquis
deputatus est" (Lk 22:37).

In the car, I crossed my three dioceses,

Saigon, Phan Thiêt, Nha Trang,

with such love for my faithful,

but none of them knows that their pastor is passing by,

the first stop on his Via Crucis.

13

But in this sea of extreme bitterness,

I feel freer than ever. I have nothing with me,

not even a penny, except my rosary and the company of
Jesus and Mary.

Along the street of captivity I prayed:

"You are my God and my all."

Jesus,

by now I can say with St. Paul:

"I, Francis, for the cause of Jesus Christ,
am now in prison for you – ego Franciscus, vinctus
Jesu Christi pro vobis" (Eph 3:1).

In the darkness of the night,

in the middle of that ocean of anxiety, of nightmares,

little by little I wake up again:

"I must confront reality.

I am in prison.

If I am waiting for the opportune moment

to do something truly great,

how many times in my life will similar occasions present
themselves!

No, I will seize the occasions that every day presents,

to fulfill ordinary actions in an extraordinary way."

Jesus,

I will not wait, I will live the present moment, filling it to
the brim with love.

A straight line is made of millions of tiny points united to
each other.

My life too is made of millions of seconds and minutes
united to each other.

I will perfectly arrange every single point,

and the line will be straight.

I will live perfectly every minute,

and my life will be holy.

The road of hope is paved with small steps of hope.

The life of hope is made of brief minutes of hope.

Like you, Jesus, who always did what was pleasing to
your Father.

Every minute I want to tell you: Jesus, I love you,

my life is ever a "new and eternal covenant" with you.

Every minute I want to sing with your Church:

Glory be to the Father and to the Son and to
the Holy Spirit . . .

Under house arrest
in Cây-Vông (Nha Trang, Central Vietnam),
August 16, 1975,
the day after the Feast of Mary's Assumption

It is true, Jesus is a demanding friend who sets high goals . . . Throw down the barriers of superficiality and fear, recognizing yourselves as "new" men and women.

John Paul II,
Message for World Youth Day XII, 1997, *n. 3*

THE SECOND LOAF
Discerning Between God and God's Works

When I was a student in Rome, a person told me: "Your greatest quality is being 'dynamic'; your greatest defect is being 'aggressive.'" In any case, I am very active; I was a scout, the chaplain of the Explorers. It is something that pushes me forward every day: to run against the clock. When I became a bishop, I had to do everything possible to strengthen and build up the Church in my diocese of Nha Trang, before the hard times came, before we fell under communist rule! I worked to increase the number of major seminarians from forty-two to one hundred forty-seven in under eight years; to increase the number of minor seminarians from two hundred to five hundred in four seminaries. I was busy organizing the ongoing formation of priests in the six dioceses of the metropolitan Church of Huê and developing and intensifying the formation of new movements for youth, lay people, and pastoral councils . . . I greatly loved my first diocese, Nha Trang.

And then, I had to leave everything to go immediately to Saigon, according to the instructions of Pope Paul VI, with no opportunity to say goodbye to all those united with me in the same ideal, the same determination, the same sharing of trials as well as joys.

That night, when I recorded my voice for a final greeting to the diocese, it was the only time in eight years when I cried, and I cried bitterly!

Then the tribulations in Saigon, the arrest. I was led back to my first diocese in Nha Trang, in the hardest captivity, so close to my bishop's residence. Morning and evening in the darkness of my cell I heard the bells of the cathedral where I spent eight years, and they tore at my heart; at night I heard the waves of the sea in front of my cell.

Then in the hull of a ship that carried fifteen hundred starving, desperate prisoners. And in the reeducation camp of Viñh-Quang, in the midst of other sad and sick prisoners, in the mountains.

Above all, the long tribulation of nine years in solitary confinement, with only two guards, a mental torture, in absolute emptiness, without work, walking in the cell from morning until nine-thirty at night so as not to be destroyed by arthritis, at the edge of insanity.

Many times I was tempted, tormented by the fact that I was forty-eight years old, the age of maturity; I had worked as a bishop for eight years, I had acquired much pastoral experience, and there I was: isolated, inactive, separated from my people, more than one thousand miles away!

One night, I heard a voice prompting me from the depths of my heart: "Why do you torment yourself so? You have to distinguish between God and God's works. Everything you have done and want to continue doing—pastoral visits, formation of seminarians, men and women religious, lay people, youth, building schools, the foyer for students, missions to evangelize non-Christians—all these are excellent works, God's works, but they are not God! If God wants you to abandon all these works, putting them in his hands, do it immediately, and have confidence in him. God will do it infinitely better than you; he will entrust his works to others who are much more capable than you. You have chosen God alone, not his works!"

I had always learned to do God's will. But this light brought me a new strength that completely changed my way of thinking and helped me overcome moments that were physically almost impossible.

At times a well-developed program has to be left unfinished; some activities begun with great enthusiasm are held up; large missions are demoted to minor activities. Maybe you are upset and discouraged, but has the Lord called you to follow him, or to follow this project or this person? Let the Lord work: He will work everything out for the best.

While I found myself in the prison of Phú-Khánh, in a cell without windows, it was extremely hot; I suffocated. I felt my lucidity lessen bit by bit until I was unconscious. At times, the light was left on day and night; at other times, it was always dark. It was so humid that mushrooms began to grow on my bed. In the darkness, I saw a hole in the bottom of the wall (to let the water run out); so

I spent one hundred days on the ground, putting my nose in front of the hole so as to breathe. When it rained, the water level rose; little insects — spiders, earthworms, millipedes — came in from outside. I let them come, I had no strength left to drive them away.

To choose God and not God's works: God wants me here and nowhere else.

When the communists loaded me into the hull of the ship *Hâi-Phóng* with another fifteen hundred prisoners to be transported north, seeing the desperation, the hate, the desire for revenge on the faces of those held under arrest, I shared their suffering, but immediately the voice called out to me again: "Choose God and not God's works." I said to myself: "In truth, Lord, here is my cathedral, here is the people of God that you have given me to take care of. I have to confirm God's presence in the midst of these desperate, miserable brothers. It is your will, so it is my choice."

Having arrived at the mountains of Vĩnh-Phú, a reeducation camp with 250 prisoners, the majority of whom were not Catholic, the voice called out to me again: "Choose God and not God's works." I said to myself, "Yes, Lord, you are sending me here to be your love among my brothers, in the midst of hunger, cold, exhausting work, humiliation, injustice. I choose you, your will; I am your missionary here."

From that moment, a new peace filled my heart and stayed with me for thirteen years. I felt my human weakness, and yet I renewed this choice in the face of difficult situations, and I never lacked peace.

When I declare, "For God and for the Church," I remain silent in the presence of God and I honestly ask myself: "Lord, am I working only for you? Are you always the essential motive of all I do? I would be ashamed to admit that there are other, stronger motives."

Choosing God and not God's works.

It is a beautiful choice, but difficult. John Paul II addresses you: "Dear young people, like the first disciples, follow Jesus! Do not be afraid of drawing close to him. Do not be afraid of the 'new life' that he offers you: He himself gives you the possibility to welcome it, to put it into practice, with the help of his grace and the gift of the Holy Spirit" (*Message for World Youth Day XII, 1997*, n. 3).

John Paul II encourages young people by showing them the example of Saint Thérèse of the Child Jesus: "Travel with her [Thérèse] the humble and simple road of Christian maturity, in the school of the Gospel. Stay with her in the 'heart' of the Church, radically living the choice for Christ" (*Message for World Youth Day XII, 1997*, n. 9).

The young boy in the Gospel made this choice, confidently offering everything, five loaves and two fish, into the hands of Jesus. Jesus accomplished "God's works," feeding five thousand men, plus women and children.

PRAYER
God and His Work

Because of your infinite love,
Lord, you have called me to follow you,
to be your son and your disciple.

Then you entrusted me with a mission
that is like no other,
but with the same objective of the others:
to be your apostle and witness.

Even so, experience has taught me
that I continue to confuse the two realities:
God and his work.

God has given me the task of his works,
some sublime,
others more modest;
some noble,
others more ordinary.

Engaged in pastoring a parish,
among youth,
in schools, among artists and workers,
in the world of the press,
of television and radio,
there I put all my ardor
committing all my abilities.
I held nothing back,
not even my life.

While I was so passionately
immersed in action,
I met the defeat
of ingratitude,
of the refusal to cooperate,
of the incomprehension of friends,
of the lack of support from superiors,
of sickness and disease,
of the lack of means . . .

It also happened that, while in the midst of complete success,
while I was the object of approval,

of eulogies and affection from all,
I was suddenly removed
and given a new role.
So here I am, seized by bewilderment.
I go groping on,
as in the dark night.

Why, Lord, do you abandon me!
I do not want to desert your work.
I have to carry your task to its completion,
to finish off the construction of the Church . . .

Why do men attack your work!
Why do they deprive it of their support?

Before your altar, next to the Eucharist,
I heard your response, Lord:
"I am the one you are following, not my work!
If I so desire, you will hand over to me the task given you.
It matters little who takes your place;
it is my affair.
You have to choose me!"

In solitary confinement
in Hanoi (North Viêt-Nam),
February 11, 1985,
Memorial of the Apparition of Mary
Immaculate at Lourdes

Know how to hear again,
in the silence of prayer,
the response of Jesus:
"Come and see."

John Paul II,
Message for World Youth Day XII, 1997, *n. 2*

THE THIRD LOAF
A Fixed Reference Point, Prayer

After my liberation, many people said to me: "Father, in prison you had a lot of time to pray." It is not as simple as you might think. The Lord let me experience the full depth of my weakness, my physical and mental fragility. Time passes slowly in prison, particularly during solitary confinement. Imagine a week, a month, two months of silence. They are terribly long, but when they are transformed into years, they become an eternity. A Viêt-Nâmese proverb says: "One day in prison is like a thousand autumns outside." There were days when, worn out by tiredness, by sickness, I did not even get so far as reciting one prayer!

A story comes to mind, the story of old Jim. Every day at twelve o'clock, Jim would come into church for only a couple of minutes then go out. The sacristan was very curious, and one day he stopped Jim and asked him:

"Why do you come here every day?"

"I come to pray."

"Impossible! How can you pray in just two minutes?"

"I am an old, ignorant man; I pray to God in my own way."

"But what do you say?"

"I say: 'Jesus, here I am; I'm Jim.' And then I leave."

The years go by. Jim gets older and falls sick. He enters a hospital, in the ward for poor people. Later on, it seems that Jim is about to die, and the priest and the nurse, a religious sister, are standing next to his bed.

"Jim, tell us: Why, from when you entered this ward, has everything changed for the better; why have the people become happier, more content, and friendlier?"

"I don't know. When I can walk, I go around here and there, visiting everyone; I greet them, talk a little bit. When I'm in bed, I call everyone over, make them all laugh, make them all happy. With Jim, they are always happy."

"But you, why are you happy?"

"When you receive a visit every day, aren't you happy?"

"Of course. But who comes to visit you? We have never seen anyone."

"When I entered this ward, I asked you for two chairs: one for you, one reserved for my guest; don't you see?"

"Who is your guest?"

"Jesus. Before, I used to go to church to visit him, now I can't anymore; so, at twelve o'clock, Jesus comes here."

"But what does Jesus say to you?"

"He says: 'Jim, here I am; I'm Jesus!' . . ."

Right before he died, old Jim smiled and gestured with his hand toward the chair next to his bed, as if to invite someone to sit down. He smiled again and closed his eyes.

When my strength failed me and I could not even say my prayers, I repeated: "Jesus, here I am; I'm Francis." Joy and consolation came, and I experienced Jesus responding: "Francis, here I am; I'm Jesus."

You will ask me: What are your favorite prayers?

In all sincerity, I love best the short and simple prayers of the Gospel:

"They have no more wine!" (Jn 2:3).

"*Magnificat . . .*" (Lk 1:46-55).

"Father, forgive them . . ." (Lk 23:34).

"*In manus tuas . . .*" (Lk 23:46).

"*Ut unum sint . . . .* That all may be one . . . ." (Jn 17:21).

"*Miserere mei peccatoris*" (Lk 18:13).

"Remember me when you come into your Kingdom" (Lk 23:42-43).

I also love to pray with the whole of God's word, with the liturgical prayers, the psalms, the canticles. I greatly love Gregorian chant, which in large part I recall by memory. Thanks to my seminary formation, these liturgical songs have entered deeply into my heart! Then there are the prayers of my native language, which my whole family prayed every evening in the family chapel, so moving, as they remind me of my childhood. Above all, the three *Ave Maria*s and the *Memorare* that my mother taught me to recite morning and evening.

As I said, I spent nine years in solitary confinement, that is, with only my two guards for company. To avoid the sicknesses due to immobility, like arthritis, I would walk all day, massaging my muscles, doing physical exercises, praying with songs like the *Miserere*, the *Te Deum*, the *Veni Creator*, and the hymn of the martyrs, *Sanctorum meritis*. These songs of the Church, inspired by God's word, provided me with a great amount of courage to follow Jesus. To value these beautiful prayers, it was necessary to experience the obscurity of prison and to become aware that our sufferings are offered for the Church's fidelity. This intention, directed to Jesus, in communion with the Holy Father and the whole Church, I sensed in an irresistible way when I repeated throughout the day: "*Per ipsum et cum ipso et in ipso . . .*"

The simple prayer of a communist — yes, a communist — comes to mind. At first he was a spy, but later he became my friend. Before my liberation, he promised me: "My house is two miles from the sanctuary of the Madonna of Lavang. I will go there to pray for you." I believed in his friendship, but I doubted that a communist would go to pray to the Madonna. Then one day, maybe six years later, while I was in solitary confinement, I received a letter from him! He wrote: "Dear friend, I promised you that I would go and pray for you to the Madonna of Lavang. I do so every Sunday, if it isn't raining. I take my bicycle when I hear the bells ringing. The basilica has been completely destroyed by the bombing, so I go to the monument of the apparition, which is still intact. I pray for you like this: Madonna, I am not a Christian; I do not know how to pray. I ask you to give Mr. Francis what he desires." I was moved to the very depths of my heart; certainly the Madonna would answer him.

In the Gospel passage that we are meditating on, before performing the miracle, before feeding the hungry people, Jesus prayed. Jesus wants to teach us: Before pastoral, social, or charitable work, it is necessary to pray.

John Paul II says: "Converse with Jesus in prayer and in listening to the Word; taste the joy of reconciliation in the sacrament of penance; receive Christ's Body and Blood in the Eucharist . . . You will discover the truth about yourselves, you will discover interior unity, and you will find the 'Thou' who heals you from anguish, from nightmares, from that savage subjectivism that does not give peace" (*Message for World Youth Day XII, 1997*, n. 3).

PRAYER
Brief Gospel Prayers

I think, Lord, that you have given me
a model of prayer.
To tell the truth, you have left only one:
the "Our Father."
It is short, concise, and dense.

Your life, Lord, is a prayer,
sincere and simple,
directed to the Father.
It so happened that your prayer was long,
without set formulas,
like the priestly prayer
after the Supper:
ardent and spontaneous.

But habitually, Jesus, the Virgin, and the Apostles
use short prayers, but beautiful ones that are linked to
their daily lives. I, who am weak and mediocre, I

love these short prayers in front of the tabernacle, at
my desk, along the street, alone. The more I repeat
them, the more I am penetrated by them. I am close
to you, Lord.

Father forgive them,
for they know not what they do.
Father, let them be one.
I am the servant of the Lord.
They have no wine.
Behold your son, behold your mother!
Remember me,
when you come into your kingdom.
Lord, what do you want me to do!
Lord, you know everything,
you know that I love you.
Lord, have pity on me,
a poor sinner.
My God, my God, why have you
abandoned me!

All of these short prayers, connected to one another,
form a life of prayer. Like a chain of discrete gestures,

of looks, of intimate words, they form a life of love. These keep us in an atmosphere of prayer without taking us away from the present task, by helping us to sanctify everything.

In solitary confinement
in Hanoi (North Viêt-Nam),
March 25, 1987,
Feast of the Annunciation

Around the Eucharistic table
the harmonious unity of the Church is
brought about and manifested,
mystery of missionary communion,
where all feel themselves to be sons
and brothers.

John Paul II,
Message for World Youth Day XII, 1997, *n. 7*

THE FOURTH LOAF
My Only Strength, the Eucharist

"Were you able to celebrate Mass in prison?" is the question that many repeatedly have asked me. And they are right: The Eucharist is the most beautiful prayer; it is the culmination of the life of Jesus. When I answer "yes," I already know the next question: "How were you able to get the bread and wine?"

When I was arrested, I had to leave immediately, with empty hands. The next day, I was allowed to request in writing the things I needed most: clothes, toothpaste. I wrote to my addressee: "Please, could you send me a bit of wine, as medicine for my bad stomach?" The faithful understood what my request meant; they sent me a small bottle of wine for Mass, labeling it "stomach medicine," and some hosts sealed in a dehumidifying torch. The police asked me:

"Do you have a bad stomach?"

"Yes."

"Here's a little medicine for you."

I will never be able to express my immense joy: Every day, with three drops of wine and one drop of water in the palm of my hand, I celebrated my Mass.

It depended on the situation, however. On the boat that brought us north, I celebrated at night and the prisoners around me received communion. At times, I had to celebrate when everyone else was bathing after calisthenics. In the reeducation camp, we were divided into groups of fifty people; we slept on common beds, having the right to fifty centimeters-width of bed space. We arranged it so that there were five Catholics with me. At nine-thirty, the lights were turned off and everyone had to sleep. It was then that I would curl up on the bed to celebrate Mass, by memory, and distribute communion, moving my hand under the mosquito netting. We made little containers from the paper of cigarette boxes to reserve the Blessed

Sacrament. Jesus in the Eucharist was always with me in my shirt pocket.

I remember what I wrote: "Entrust yourself to one power, the Holy Eucharist, the Body and Blood of the Lord which was given that you may live: 'I came that they may have life and have it abundantly' (Jn 10:10). As the Israelites were fed by manna during their journey to the Promised Land, so too you will be nourished by the Eucharist as you travel along the Road of Hope to your heavenly homeland (cf. Jn 6:50)" (*The Road of Hope*, n. 983).

In the reeducation camps, a session of indoctrination took place every week in which the whole camp had to participate. During the break, I and my Catholic companions took advantage of the opportunity to give a little container to each of the other four groups of prisoners: They all knew that Jesus was among them, that he is the one who cures all their physical and mental suffering. At night, the prisoners would take turns keeping adoration; Jesus helped in a tremendous way with his silent presence. Many Christians regained the fervor of their faith during these days, and Buddhists and other non-Christians converted. The strength of the love of Jesus is irresistible. The darkness of prison became light, the seed germinated underground during the storm.

I offer Mass together with the Lord: When I distribute communion, I give myself together with the Lord to make myself food for everyone. This means that I am always totally at the service of others.

Every time that I offer Mass I have the opportunity to extend my hands and nail myself to the Cross with Jesus, to drink with him the bitter cup.

Every day, reciting and listening to the words of the consecration, I confirm with all my heart and with all my soul a new covenant, an eternal covenant between me and Jesus, through his blood mixed with mine (1 Cor 11:23-25).

Jesus started a revolution from the Cross. Your revolution has to begin from the Eucharistic table and from there be carried forward. In this way, you will be able to renew humanity.

I spent nine years in solitary confinement. During this period, I celebrated Mass every day around three in the afternoon: the hour of Jesus agonizing on the Cross. I was alone; I could sing my Mass as I wished: in Latin, French, Viêt-Nâmese . . . I always carried with me the little container with the Blessed Sacrament: "You in me and I in you."

They were the most beautiful Masses of my life.

In the evening, from nine to ten o'clock, I had an hour of adoration during which I sang the *Lauda Sion*, the *Pange Lingua*, the *Adoro Te*, the *Te Deum*, and songs in Viêt-Nâmese — all despite the noise of the loudspeaker that blared propaganda at me every day from five o'clock in the morning till eleven-thirty at night. I felt a singular peace of spirit and of heart and the joy, the serenity of the company of Jesus, Mary, and Joseph. I sang the *Salve Regina*, the *Salve Mater*, the *Alma Redemptoris Mater*, the *Regina Caeli* . . . in union with the universal Church. Despite the accusations, the calumnies against the Church, I sang the *Tu es Petrus*, the *Oremus pro Pontifice nostro*, the *Christus vincit.* Just as Jesus relieved the hunger of the crowd that followed him in the desert, in the Eucharist it is he himself who continues to be the food of eternal life.

In the Eucharist, we announce the death of Jesus, and we proclaim his resurrection. They are moments of infinite sadness; how do I do it? By looking at Jesus crucified and abandoned on the Cross. To human eyes, the life of Jesus was a failure, useless, frustrated, but, in God's eyes, on the Cross Jesus has accomplished the most important action of his life, because he poured out his blood to save the world. How greatly Jesus was united to God when, on the Cross, he could no longer preach, cure the sick, visit people, perform miracles, but remain in absolute immobility!

Jesus is my first example of radical love, for the Father and for souls. Jesus gave everything: *"In finem dilexit"* (Jn 13:1), up to the *"consummatum est"* (Jn 19:30). And the Father loved the world *"ut Filium suum unigenitum traderet"* (Jn 3:16). To give himself as bread to be eaten *"pro mundi vita"* (Jn 6:51).

Jesus said: "*Misereor super turbam*" (Mt 15:32). The multiplication of the loaves is an announcement, a sign of the Eucharist that Jesus will soon institute.

My dear young people, listen to the Holy Father: "Jesus lives among us in the Eucharist . . . amidst the uncertainties and distractions of daily life, imitate the disciples on the road to Emmaus . . . Call upon Jesus, so that along the many roads to Emmaus of our times he will remain with you. Let him be your strength, him your point of reference, him your everlasting hope" (*John Paul II, Message for World Youth Day XII, 1997*, n. 7).

PRAYER
Present and Past

Jesus beloved,

this evening, in the back of my cell,

without light, without a window, stiflingly hot,

I think with overwhelming nostalgia of my pastoral life.

Eight years as bishop, in this residence,

only two kilometers from my prison cell,

on the same street, on the same shore...

I hear the waves of the Pacific, the bells of the cathedral.

– Once I used to celebrate with a gold-plated paten and
   chalice,

now your blood in the palm of my hand.

– Once I used to travel the world for conferences and
   meetings,

now I am confined in a narrow cell, without a window.

– Once I used to go and visit you in the tabernacle,
now I carry you with me, night and day, in my pocket.

– Once I used to celebrate Mass in front of thousands
    of faithful,
now in the darkness of night, giving communion under
    mosquito netting.

– Once I used to preach spiritual exercises to priests, to
    religious, to lay people . . .
now a priest, also a prisoner, preaches to me the Exercises
    of Saint Ignatius through a crack in the wood.

– Once I used to give solemn benediction with the
    Blessed Sacrament in the cathedral,
now I have eucharistic adoration every evening at nine
    o'clock, in silence, singing softly the *Tantum Ergo*,
    the *Salve Regina*, and concluding with this short
    prayer: "Lord, now I am content to accept everything
    from your hands: all the sadness, the suffering, the
    anguish, even my death. Amen."

I am happy, here, in this cell,
where on the mat white mushrooms are growing,

because you are with me,
because you want me to live here with you.

I have spoken a lot in my lifetime,
now I speak no more.
It is your turn, Jesus, to speak to me.
I am listening to you: What have you whispered to me!
Is it a dream!
You do not speak to me of the past, of the present,
you do not speak of my sufferings, anguish . . .
You speak to me of your plans, of my mission.

So I sing of your mercy,
in darkness, in my weakness, in my annihilation.

I accept my cross
and I plant it, with my own two hands,
in my heart.

If you were to permit me to choose, I would not change,
because you are with me!
I am not afraid anymore, I have understood,

I am following you in your passion
and in your resurrection.

In solitary confinement,
the prison of Phú Khánh (Central Viêt-Nam),
October 7, 1976,
Feast of the Holy Rosary

Dear young people,
you are called to be believable
witnesses of Christ's Gospel,
which renews all things....
"Love one another" (Jn 15:35).

John Paul II,
Message for World Youth Day XII, 1997, *n. 8*

THE FIFTH LOAF
To Love Until Unity, the Testimony of Jesus

One night when I was sick, in the prison of Phú Khánh, I saw a policeman walk by and I shouted: "For goodness' sake, I am very sick; please give me some medicine!" He responded: "There is no goodness here, nor love; there is only responsibility."

This was the atmosphere we breathed in prison.

When I was put into solitary confinement, I was initially entrusted to a group of five guards, two of whom always accompanied me. The wardens would change them every two weeks, so that they would not become "contaminated" by me. Later they decided not to change them anymore, otherwise they would all be contaminated!

At first, the guards did not speak to me; they responded only with a curt "yes" or "no." It was truly sad; I wanted to be kind, courteous with them, but it was impossible; they avoided speaking to me. I had no presents to give them: I was a prisoner, even all my clothes were stamped with big letters "*cai-tao,*" that is, "reeducation camp." What was I supposed to do?

One night, a thought came to me: "Francis, you are still very rich. You have the love of Christ in your heart. Love them as Jesus has loved you." The next day I began to love them, to love Jesus in them, smiling, exchanging kind words. I began to tell them stories of my travels overseas, of how people lived in America, Canada, Japan, the Philippines, Singapore, France, Germany . . . the economy, the freedom, the technology. This stimulated their curiosity and pushed them to ask me about many things. Little by little, we became friends. They wanted to learn foreign languages: French, English . . . My guards became my students! The atmosphere of the prison greatly changed, the quality of our relationships was greatly improved, even up to the police chiefs. When they saw the sincerity of my relationship with the guards, they not only asked me to continue helping them study foreign languages, but they also sent new students to study with me.

One day one of the head guards asked me a question:

"What do you think of the newspaper *The Catholic?*"

"This newspaper does good neither for Catholics nor for the government, rather it has enlarged the gulf of separation. Because it expresses itself badly; they use religious vocabulary wrongly, and they speak offensively."

"How can we remedy the situation?"

"First, you have to understand exactly what the word means, the religious terminology."

"Could you help us?"

"Yes, I propose writing a lexicon of religious language, from A to Z; when you have a free moment, I will explain it to you. I hope that in this way you can understand better the structure, the history, the development of the Church, her activities . . ."

They gave me paper; I wrote this lexicon of fifteen hundred words, in French, English, Italian, Latin, Spanish, and Chinese, with the explanation in Viêt-Nâmese. Thus, little by little, with the explanation, with my response to questions about the Church, and also with my acceptance of criticism, this document became a "practical catechism." They were very curious to know what a patriarch or an abbot is; what the difference is between Orthodox, Catholic, Anglican, Lutheran; where the finances of the Vatican come from.

This systematic dialogue from A to Z helped correct many mistakes, many preconceived notions; every day it became more interesting, even fascinating.

During this time, I heard that a group of twenty young members of the police were studying Latin with a former catechist, so as to be able to understand ecclesiastical documents. One of my guards belonged to this group; one day he asked if I could teach him a song in Latin.

"There are many, and so beautiful," I responded.

"You sing; I'll choose," he responds.

I sang the *Salve Regina,* the *Veni Creator,* the *Ave Maris Stella.* Can you guess which song he chose? The *Veni Creator.*

I can't tell you how moving it was to hear a young communist police officer go down the wooden staircase around seven o'clock to go to calisthenics and then clean up while singing the *Veni Creator*—right there in the prison!

When there is love, one feels joy and peace, because Jesus is there among us. "You need to wear only one uniform and speak only one language: that of love" (*The Road of Hope,* n. 984).

One rainy day in the mountains of Viñh-Phú, in the prison of Viñh-Quang, I had to chop wood. I asked the guard:

"Can I ask you a favor?"

"What? Can I help you?"

"I would like to cut a piece of wood in the form of a cross."

"Don't you know that religious symbols are strictly prohibited?"

"I know, but we are friends, and I promise to hide it."

"It would be extremely dangerous for both of us."

"Close your eyes; I will do it now, and I will be very cautious."

He went away and left me alone. I cut the cross and kept it hidden in a piece of soap until my liberation. With a metal covering, this piece of wood has become my pectoral cross.

In another prison, I asked my guard—who had already become my friend—for a piece of electric wire. He was surprised:

"At the police academy, I learned that when a prisoner wants some electric wire, it means that he wants to commit suicide."

I explained: "Catholic priests do not commit suicide."

"But what are you going to do with electric wire?"

"I would like to make a small chain so I can wear my cross."

"How can you make a chain with electric wire? That's impossible!"

"If you bring me two little pincers, I will show you."

"It's too dangerous!"

"But we are friends!"

He hesitated, then he said, "I will answer in three days."

After three days, he said to me, "It is hard to refuse you anything. I thought to myself: This evening I will bring two small pincers; from seven o'clock to eleven, we have to finish this work. I will let the other guard go and see 'Hanoi by Night.' If he were to see us, he would make a report dangerous for both of us."

We cut the electric wire into pieces the size of matches, we linked them up . . . and the chain was finished before eleven.

I wear this cross and this chain every day, not because they are reminders of prison, but because they indicate my profound conviction, a constant reference point for me: Only Christian love can change hearts—not weapons, threats, or the media.

It was very difficult for my guards to understand how one can forgive, love one's enemies, reconcile oneself with them.

"Do you really love us?"

"Yes, I sincerely love you."

"Even when we treat you so badly? When you suffer because you have been in prison for so many years without a trial?"

"Think about the years we have lived together. I really love you!"

"When you are free, you won't send your people to take revenge on us and our families?"

"No, I will continue to love you, even if you want to kill me."

"But why?"

"Because Jesus has taught me how to love you. If I do not, I am no longer worthy to be called a Christian."

There is not enough time to tell you other very moving stories, all of them testimonies of the liberating power of the love of Jesus.

In the Gospel, Jesus, seeing the crowd that has followed him for three days, said, "*Misereor super turbam*" (Mt 15:32), "They are like sheep without a shepherd" (cf. Mk 6:34). In the most dramatic moments in prison, when I was on the verge of exhaustion, without strength enough even to pray or to meditate, I looked for a way to sum up the essence of my prayer, the message of Jesus, and I used this phrase: "I am living the testimony of Jesus." That is, loving others as Jesus has loved me, in forgiveness, in mercy, until unity, as he prayed: "May they all be one. Father, may they be one in us, as you are in me and I am in you" (Jn 17:21). I often prayed: "I am living the testament of the love of Jesus." I want to be the boy who offered everything he had. It is nothing, five loaves and two fish, but it is "everything" that he had, given up to be "an instrument of the love of Jesus."

Dear young people, Pope John Paul II sends out his message to you: "You will find Jesus where men suffer and hope: in the little villages spread throughout the continents, apparently on the margins of history, as Nazareth was; in the immense metropolises where millions of human beings often live as strangers. Jesus is at your side . . . his face is that of the poorest, of the marginalized, victims not infrequently of an unjust model of development that puts profit in the first place and makes man a means instead of an end . . . . Jesus lives among those who invoke him without having known him. Jesus lives among the men and women 'honored by the name of Christian,' but, on the eve of the third millennium, every day the duty to repair the scandal of the division of Christians becomes more urgent" (*Message for World Youth Day XII, 1997*, n. 5).

The biggest mistake we can make as Christians is not to be aware that others are Christ. All too many will not discover this until the last day.

Jesus was abandoned on the Cross, and in the same way, he is still abandoned in every brother and sister who suffers, in every corner of the world. Charity has no boundaries; if it has boundaries, it is no longer charity.

PRAYER
Consecration

Father almighty, immense in love, source of my hope and of my joy:

1 – "All that is mine is yours" (Lk 15:31). "Ask and you will be given" (Mt 7:7).

Father, firmly I believe it: Your love surpasses infinity. How can the love of your children compete with yours?

Oh! The immensity of your fatherly love! All that is yours is mine. You have instructed me to pray in sincerity. So I place my trust in you, Father overflowing with goodness.

2 – "All is grace." (St. Thérèse de Lisieux) "Your Father knows what you need" (Mt 6:8).

Father, firmly I believe it: You have ordered all things for our greater good, from all time. You never cease guiding my life. You accompany each of my steps. What shall I be able to fear? Lying face down, I adore your holy will. I put myself totally into your hands; it is on your behalf that everything comes to pass. I, who am your son, believe that all is grace.

3 – "I can do all things in him who strengthens me" (Phil 4:13). "To the praise of his glory" (Eph 1:6).

Father, firmly I believe it:

Nothing surpasses the power of your providence. Your love is infinite, and I want to accept everything with a joyful heart, to perpetuate praise and recognition. United to the Virgin Mary, joining their voices to those of all the nations, St. Joseph and the angels sing God's glory forever and ever. Amen.

4 – "Do all things for God's glory" (1 Cor 10:31). "Thy will be done" (Mt 6:10).

Father, firmly and without hesitation I believe that you work and act in me. I am the object of your love and tenderness. Do with me whatever can give you even more praise!

I ask for nothing but your glory – this is enough for my satisfaction and happiness. This is my greatest aspiration, my soul's most pressing desire.

5 – "Everything for the mission! Everything for the Church!"

Father, firmly I believe it: You have entrusted me

with a mission, completely sealed by your love. You prepare the way for me. I do not stop purifying myself and anchoring myself in my resolution.

Yes, I have decided: I will become a silent offering. I will serve as an instrument in the hands of the Father. I will consume my sacrifice, moment by moment, out of love for the Church: "Here I am; I am ready!"

6 – "I have ardently desired to eat this Passover with you" (Lk 22:15). "All is finished" (Jn 19:30).

Most loving Father! United to the holy sacrifice that I continue to offer, I kneel down in this instant, and for you, I pronounce the word that springs from my heart: "Sacrifice."

A sacrifice that accepts humiliation as glory, a joyful sacrifice, an integral sacrifice . . . It sings my hope and all my love.

In the prison of Phú Khánh
(Central Viêt-Nam),
September 1, 1976,
Feast of the Holy Viêt-Nâmese Martyrs

To Mary I entrust ... the hopes and expectations of the young people who, in every corner of the planet, repeat with her: "Behold, the hand-maid of the Lord, may it be done unto me according to thy word" (Lk 1:38) ... [and are] ready then to announce to their contemporaries, like the apostles: "We have found the Messiah!" (Jn 1:41).

John Paul II,
Message for World Youth Day XII, 1997, *n. 10*

THE FIRST FISH
Immaculate Mary, My First Love

"Immaculate Mary, my first love": This is the thought of John Mary Vianney, the Curé d'Ars. I read it in a book by François Trochu when I was in the minor seminary.

My mother instilled in my heart this love for Mary from when I was just a child. My grandmother, every evening after family prayers, prayed another rosary. When I asked her why, she replied "I say a rosary praying to Mary for priests." Even if they did not know how to read or write, it is these mothers, these grandmothers, who shaped the vocation in our hearts.

Mary has a special role in my life. I was arrested on August 15, 1975, the Feast of Mary's Assumption. I left in the police car empty-handed, without a penny in my pocket, only with my rosary, and I was at peace. That night, on the three hundred-mile-long road, I prayed the *Memorare* many times.

You will ask how Mary helped me overcome the many trials of my life. I will tell you some episodes that are still vivid in my memory.

When I was a young priest studying in Rome in September 1957, I made a pilgrimage to the grotto of Lourdes to pray to the Madonna. At that time, I had a "presentiment": It seemed to me that the words addressed to St. Bernadette by the Immaculate Lady were also directed to me: "Bernadette, I do not promise you joy and consolation on this earth but rather trials and suffering." Not without fear, I accepted this message. After graduating, I returned to Viêt-Nam as a professor and then rector of the seminary of Huê; afterward, I was vicar general of that same archdiocese and then bishop of Nha Trang in 1967. One could say that my pastoral ministry was crowned with success, thanks be to God.

I returned other times to pray at the grotto of Lourdes. I often wondered: "Perhaps the words directed to Bernadette are not for me? Are my daily crosses unbearable? In any case, I am ready to do God's will."

Then the year 1975 came and with it my arrest, prison, solitary confinement, more than thirteen years in captivity. Now I understand that the Madonna wanted to prepare me in 1957! "I do not promise you joy and consolation in this life but trials and suffering." Every day I understand more intimately the deep meaning of this message, and I confidently abandon myself into Mary's hands.

When the physical and moral miseries in prison became too heavy and they kept me from praying, it was then that I prayed the *Ave Maria*, repeating that prayer hundreds of times over, as I offered everything into the hands of the Immaculate, praying to her to distribute graces to all who have need of them in the Church. Everything with Mary, through Mary, and in Mary.

I did not pray to Mary only to ask for her intercession, but I often asked her: "Mother, what can I do for you? I am ready to fulfill your orders, to carry out your desires for the kingdom of Jesus." Then an immense peace would invade my heart; I was no longer afraid.

While I prayed to Mary, I did not forget St. Joseph, her spouse: This is a desire of Mary and Jesus, who have a great love for St. Joseph, with his very special titles.

Mary Immaculate did not abandon me. She accompanied me the whole way along my march through the darkness of prison. In those days of unspeakable trials, I prayed to Mary with complete simplicity and trust: "Mother, if you see that I can no longer be useful to your Church, grant me the grace to consume my life in prison. But if instead you know that I will still be able to be useful to your Church, let me leave prison on one of your feast days!"

One rainy day, while I was preparing my lunch, I heard the guards' telephone ring. "Maybe this call is for me!" I thought. "After all, today is November 21st, the feast of Mary's Presentation in the Temple!"

Five minutes later, my guard arrived:

"Mr. Thuan, have you eaten?"

"Not yet, I am still getting it ready."

"After you eat, get dressed up and you will go see the chief."

"Who is the chief?"

"I don't know, but they told me to tell you. Good luck!"

A car took me to a building where I met the minister of the Interior, that is, of the police. After some polite greetings, he asked me:

"Do you wish to express any desires?"

"Yes, I want to be freed."

"When?"

"Today."

He was very surprised. I explained:

"Your Excellency, I have been in prison quite a long time: for three pontificates, those of Paul VI, John Paul I, and John Paul II, and, in addition, under four general secretaries of the Soviet Communist Party: Brezhnev, Andropov, Chernenko, and Gorbachev!"

He began to laugh and to nod his head:

"That's true, that's true!"

And turning to his secretary, he said:

"Do what is necessary to fulfill his desire."

All of a sudden, the wardens needed only some time to take care of the formalities, but in that moment, I thought:

"Today is the feast of the Madonna, the Presentation. Mary is setting me free. Thank you, Mary."

The moment when I feel myself most especially to be Mary's son is during the holy Mass, when I say the words of the consecration. I am identified with Jesus, *in persona Christi*.

You ask, who is Mary in my radical choice for Jesus? On the Cross, Jesus said to John: "Behold your mother!" (Jn 19:29). After the institution of the Eucharist, the Lord could not have left me anything greater than his mother.

For me, Mary is like a living Gospel, portable, widely available, more accessible than the lives of the saints.

For me, Mary is my mother, given to me by Jesus. The first reaction of a child when afraid, in difficulty, or suffering, is to cry out: "Mamma, mamma!" This word is everything for the child.

Mary lived completely for Jesus. Her mission was to share his work of redemption. All her glory comes from him; that is, my life will not produce anything if I separate myself from Jesus.

Mary did not worry only about Jesus, but she showed her solicitude also for Elizabeth, for John, and for the couple at Cana.

I love very much the words of St. Thérèse of the Child Jesus: "I want so much to be a priest, so that I can be able to talk of Mary to everyone."

At first I used to run to Mary, Mother of Perpetual Help; now I listen to Mary who says to me: "Do whatever he tells you" (Jn 2:5). Often I ask Mary: "Mother, what can I do for you?" I always keep on being a child, but a responsible child who knows how to share the concerns of his mother.

Mary's life can be summed up in three words: *Ecce, Fiat, Magnificat.*

"Behold the handmaid of the Lord": *Ecce* (Lk 1:38).

"May it be done unto me according to your word": *Fiat* (Lk 1:38).

"My soul magnifies the Lord": *Magnificat* (Lk 1:46).

PRAYER
Mary, My Mother

Mary,

My Mother,

Mother of Jesus, our Mother,

to feel myself united to Jesus

and to all men, my brothers,

I want to call you Our Mother.

Come to live in me, with Jesus your most beloved Son,

this message of total renewal,

in silence and in watching,

in prayer and in offering,

in communion with the Church and with the Trinity,

in the fervor of your Magnificat,

united to Joseph, your most holy spouse,

in your humble and loving work to bring to fulfillment
the testament of Jesus,

in your love for Jesus and Joseph,

for the Church and humanity,

in your faith, unshakable in the midst of so many trials

endured for the Kingdom,
in your hope, which acts uninterruptedly,
of constructing a new world of justice and of peace,
of happiness and of true tenderness,
in the perfection of your virtues,
in the Holy Spirit,
to become a witness of the Good News,
apostle of the Gospel.

In me, O Mother, continue to work,
to pray,
to love,
to sacrifice me;
continue to fulfill the Father's will,
continue to be the Mother of humanity.
Continue to live the passion and the resurrection of Jesus.
O Mother, I consecrate myself to you, everything to you,
    now and forever.
Living in your spirit and in Joseph's,
I will live in the spirit of Jesus,
with Jesus, Joseph, the angels, the saints, and all souls.
I love you, O our Mother,
and I will share your effort,

your preoccupation and your combat
for the Kingdom of the Lord Jesus.
Amen.

In solitary confinement
Hanoi (North Viêt-Nam),
January 1, 1986,
Solemnity of Mary, the Holy Mother of God

A message that you, young people of today, are called to welcome and to shout out to your companions:
"Man is loved by God!
Man is loved by God!
This is the simple and overwhelming announcement that the Church owes to man" (Christifideles Laici, *n. 34*).

John Paul II,
Message for World Youth Day XII, 1997, *n. 9*

THE SECOND FISH
I Have Chosen Jesus

I have spoken to you about my experiences following Jesus so as to find him, to live beside him, and thereby carry his message to everyone.

You will ask me: How can one practice complete union with Jesus in a life tossed around by so many changes? I have not hidden it from you, but for clarity I will rewrite it, my secret! (cf. *The Road of Hope*, nn. 979-1001).

At the beginning of each paragraph I put a number: one through twenty-four; I wanted to make it correspond to the hours in a day. In every number, I repeated the word "one": one revolution, one campaign, one slogan, one strength . . . They are very practical things. If we live twenty-four out of twenty-four hours radically for Jesus, we will be saints. They are twenty-four stars that light up our road of hope.

I am not going to explain these thoughts to you; I invite you to meditate on them calmly, as if it were Jesus speaking sweetly, intimately to your hearts. Do not be afraid to listen to him, to speak with him. Do not hesitate; reread them once a week. You will find that the grace will shine forth, transforming your lives.

We will conclude with the prayer "I Have Chosen Jesus"; be sure to note the fourteen steps in the life of Jesus.

1. You want one revolution: to renew the world. You will be able to fulfill this precious and noble mission that God has entrusted to you, only with "the power of the Holy Spirit." Every day, there where you live, prepare a new Pentecost.

2. Commit yourself to one campaign, the goal of which is to make everyone happy. Sacrifice yourself continually, with Jesus, so as to bring peace to souls, development and prosperity to peoples. This will be your spirituality, discrete and concrete at the same time.

3. Stay faithful to the ideal of the apostle: "Give your life for your brothers." In fact, "No one has greater love than this" (Jn 15:13). Expend, without rest, all your energies and be ready to give yourself to conquer your neighbor for God.

4. Shout only one slogan: "All one," that is, unity among Catholics, unity among Christians, and unity among nations. "As the Father and the Son are one" (cf. Jn 17:22-23).

5. Believe in only one strength: the Eucharist, the body and blood of the Lord that will give you life. "I have come that they may have life, and have it to the full" (Jn 10:10). As the manna nourished the Israelites on their journey to the promised land, so the Eucharist will nourish you on your road of hope (Jn 6:50).

6. Wear only one uniform and speak only one language: charity. Charity is the sign that you are a disciple of the Lord (cf. Jn 13:35). It is the least expensive brand name but the hardest one to find. Charity is the principal "language."

St. Paul considered it more precious than "speaking the languages of men and angels" (1 Cor 13:1). It will be the only language left in Heaven.

7. Stick firmly to only one guiding principle: prayer. No one is stronger than the person who prays, because the Lord has promised to grant everything to those who pray. When you are united in prayer, the Lord is present among you (Mt 18:20). I recommend this to you with all my heart: In addition to time for "official" prayer, withdraw every day for an hour—or, even better, for two hours, if you can—for personal prayer. I assure you that it will not be wasted time! In my experience, in all these years, I have seen the words of St. Teresa of Avila confirmed: "Whoever does not pray does not need the Devil to lead him off the path: He will throw himself into Hell."

8. Observe only one rule: the Gospel. This constitution is superior to all others. It is the rule that Jesus left to his Apostles (cf. Mt 4:23). It is not difficult, complicated, or legalistic like the oth-

ers: On the contrary, it is dynamic, gentle, and stimulating for your soul. A saint far away from the Gospel is a false saint!

9. Loyally follow only one leader: Jesus Christ and his representatives—the Holy Father, the bishops, successors of the Apostles (cf. Jn 20:22-23). Live and die for the Church, just as Christ did. Do not believe that only dying for the Church requires sacrifice; living for the Church also requires much sacrifice.

10. Cultivate a special love for Mary. St. John Mary Vianney used to confide: "After Jesus, my first love is Mary." If you listen to Mary, you will not lose your way; whatever you undertake in her name will not fail. Honor her and you will gain eternal life.

11. Your only wisdom will be the science of the Cross (cf. 1 Cor 2:2). Look to the Cross and you will find the solution to all the problems that assail you. If the Cross is the criterion of your choices and your decisions, your soul will be at peace.

12. Keep only one ideal: to be turned toward God the Father, a Father who is all love. The whole life of the Lord, his every thought and action, had only one goal: "The world must be brought to know that I love the Father and that I am doing exactly what the Father has told me" (Jn 14:31), and "I always do what pleases him" (Jn 8:29).

13. There is only one evil that you must fear: sin. When the court of the eastern emperor gathered to discuss what punishment to inflict on St. John Chrysostom for his frank denunciation of the empress, the following possibilities were suggested:

    a) Throw him in prison: "But," they said, "there he would have the opportunity to pray and suffer for the Lord, as he has always desired."

    b) Exile him: "But, for him, there is no place where the Lord does not live."

    c) Condemn him to death: "But then he will become a martyr and will satisfy his aspiration to go to the Lord."

"None of these possibilities will constitute a punishment for him, on the contrary, he will accept them with joy."

d) There is only one thing that he fears greatly and hates with his whole being — sin: "But it would be impossible to force him to commit a sin!"

   If you fear sin alone, your strength will be unequalled.

14. Cultivate only one desire: "Thy Kingdom come; Thy will be done on earth as it is in Heaven" (Mt 6:10). So that throughout the earth all nations will know God as he is known in Heaven; so that on this earth everyone will begin to love one another as in Heaven; so that also on this earth there will be the beatitude that there is in Heaven. Make the effort to spread this desire. Begin now to bring the happiness of Heaven to everyone in this world.

15. Only one thing is lacking: "Go and sell everything you own and give the money to the poor, and you will have treasure in Heaven; then

come, follow me" (Mk 10:21). That is, you have to make up your mind once and for all. The Lord wants volunteers free from every attachment.

16. For your apostolate, use the one effective means: personal contact. With this, you enter into the lives of others, you understand them and love them. Personal relationships are more effective than preaching and books. Contact between people and "heart to heart" exchange are the secret of your work's endurance and your success.

17. There is only one truly important thing: "Mary chose the better part" when she sat at the Lord's feet (cf. Lk 10: 41-42). If you do not have an interior life, if Jesus is not truly the soul of your activity, then . . . but you know it well, no need to repeat it.

18. Your only food: "The Father's will" (Jn 4:34); it is with this that you must live and grow, your actions must proceed from God's will. This is like a food that makes you live stronger and happier; if you live far away from God's will, you will die.

19. For you, the most beautiful moment is the present moment (cf. Mt 6:34; Jas 4:13-15). Live it full of love for God. Your life will be marvelously beautiful if it is like a huge crystal of millions of such moments. Do you see how easy it is?

20. Have one "*magna carta*": the beatitudes (Mt 5:3-12) that Jesus announced in the Sermon on the Mount. Live them to the full: You will experience a happiness that you will then be able to communicate to everyone you meet.

21. Have only one important objective: your duty. It is not important if it is large or small, because you are collaborating with the heavenly Father. He has established this as the work you must accomplish to carry out his plan for history (cf. Lk 2:49; Jn 17:4). Many people invent for themselves complicated ways to practice virtue and then complain of the difficulties that result, but fulfilling the duty of one's state in life is the most secure and simplest way of asceticism that you can follow.

22. Have only one way to become a saint: God's grace and your will (cf. 1 Cor 15:10). God will never leave you lacking in his grace, but is your will strong enough?

23. Only one reward: God himself. When God asked St. Thomas Aquinas: "You have written well of me, Thomas: What reward do you want?", St. Thomas responded: "Only you, Lord!"

24. . . . You have one homeland.

The bell rings, grave, deep,
Viêt-Nam prays.
The bell rings still, stabbing, charge of emotion,
Viêt-Nam weeps.
The bell clangs again, vibrant, pathetic,
Viêt-Nam triumphs.
The bell tolls, crystalline,
Viêt-Nam hopes.

You have a homeland, Viêt-Nam,
A country so beloved, through the centuries.
It is your pride, your joy.
Love her mountains and her rivers,
Her brocade and satin landscapes.
Love her glorious history,
Love her hard-working people,
Love her heroic defenders.

The raging rivers run,
As runs her people's blood.
Her mountains are high,
But higher still the bones there that pile up.
The land is narrow but vast her ambition,
O little country much renowned!

Help your homeland with all your soul,
Be faithful to her,
Defend her with your body and blood,
Build her up with your heart and mind,
Share the joy of your brothers,
and the sadness of your people.

One Viêt-Nam
One people
One soul
One culture
One tradition

O Viêt-Nâmese Catholic,

Love a thousand times your homeland!
The Lord teaches you, the Church asks you, "May
the love of your country be fully one with the
blood that runs through your veins."

Someone asked Chiara Lubich: "What is your
secret? How do you attract so many people?" she
replied "I don't think about attracting anyone; I follow
Jesus with my whole heart and the others follow me."

PRAYER
I Have Chosen Jesus

Lord Jesus,
on the path of hope,
of two thousand years,
your love, like a wave,
has lifted many pilgrims.
These you have loved with a throbbing love,
with their thoughts, their words, their actions.
You have loved with a heart
stronger than temptation,
stronger than suffering and even than death.
These have been your word in the world.
Their lives have been a revolution
that has renewed the face of the Church.

Contemplating, from my childhood,
these shining examples,
I conceived a dream:
to offer you my whole life,

my only life that I am living,
for an eternal and unalterable ideal.
I have decided!
If I fulfill your will
you will achieve this ideal
and I will throw myself into this wonderful adventure.

I have chosen you,
I have never had regrets.
I hear you say to me:
"Remain in me. Remain in my love!"
But how can I remain in another?
Only love can achieve
this extraordinary mystery.
I understand that you want my whole life.
"Everything! And for your love!"

On the path of hope
I follow your every step.
Your wandering steps to the stable in Bethlehem.
Your worried steps on the road to Egypt.
Your rapid steps to the house of Nazareth.

Your joyful steps to go out with your parents to the
Temple.

Your weary steps in the thirty years of work.

Your solicitous steps in the three years of preaching the
Good News.

Your hurried steps to seek out the lost sheep.

Your sorrowful steps on entering Jerusalem.

Your solitary steps in front of the Praetorium.

Your steps weighed down under the Cross on the road to
Calvary.

Your failed steps, dead and buried in a tomb not your
own.

Stripped of everything,

without clothes, without a friend.

Abandoned even by your Father,

but always submissive to your Father.

Lord Jesus,

on my knees,

toward you, for you, in front of the tabernacle,

I understand:

I would not be able to choose another road,

another, happier road,

even if by appearances

it seemed more glorious –

for you, eternal friend,

only friend of my life,

you are not present there.

In you is all of Heaven with the Trinity,

the whole world and all humanity.

Your sufferings are mine.

Mine are all the sufferings of men.

Mine are all things in which there is neither peace, nor
joy,

nor beauty, nor comfort, nor friendliness.

Mine are all the sadness, the delusions,

the divisions, the abandonment, the disgraces.

To me let come whatever is yours, because you have
borne all,

whatever is in my brothers, because you are in them.

I firmly believe in you,

because you have taken the steps of triumph.

"Be courageous. I have overcome the world."

You have told me: Walk with giant steps.

Go all over the world,

proclaim the Good News,

dry the tears of sorrow,

reassure discouraged hearts,

reunite divided hearts,

embrace the world with the ardor of your love,

do away with what must be destroyed,

leave only truth, justice, love.

But Lord, I know my weakness!

Free me from egoism, from my securities,

so that I no longer fear the suffering that torments,

unworthy of being an apostle.

Render me strong for the adventure.

Make me not worry about the world's wisdom.

I accept being treated as someone crazy,

for Jesus, Mary, and Joseph . . .

I want to put myself to the test,

ready for every consequence,

heedless of the consequences,

because you have taught me

to confront every adventure.

If you send me to the cross,

I will let myself be crucified.

If you send me into the silence
of your tabernacle until the end of time,
I will enter therein with adventurous steps.
I will lose everything,
but I will stay with you.
Your love will be there
to flood my heart
with love for all.
My happiness will be complete . . .
It is for this that I repeat:
I have chosen you.
I want nothing except you
and your glory.

Under house arrest
in Giang-xá (North Viêt-Nam),
March 19, 1980,
Solemnity of St. Joseph, Husband of Mary